FARM ANIMALS

COW

Katie Dicker

A⁺

Smart Apple Media

Published by Smart Apple Media,
an imprint of Black Rabbit Books
P.O. Box 3263, Mankato, Minnesota, 56002
www.blackrabbitbooks.com

Printed in the United States of America,
at Corporate Graphics in North Mankato, Minnesota.

Designed by Helen James
Edited by Mary-Jane Wilkins

Library of Congress Cataloging-in-Publication Data

Dicker, Katie.
 Cow / Katie Dicker.
    p. cm. -- (Farm animals)
 Includes index.
 ISBN 978-1-62588-019-2
 1. Cows--Juvenile literature. 2. Dairy cattle--Juvenile literature. I. Title.
 SF239.5.D53 2014
 636.2--dc23

                        2013000057

Photo acknowledgements
l = left, r = right, t = top, b = bottom
title page Eric Isselée/Shutterstock, page 3 smereka/Shutterstock,
5 Digital Vision/Thinkstock; 6 val lawless/Shutterstock; 7 Hemera/
Thinkstock; 8 Niels Quist/Shutterstock; 9t aodaodaodaod,
b Dmitry Kalinovsky/both Shutterstock; 10 Monkey Business Images/
Shutterstock; 11 Igorsky/Shutterstock; 12 David Maska/Shutterstock;
13 Hemera/Thinkstock; 14 Christian Musat/Shutterstock;
15 iStockphoto/Thinkstock; 16 Wasan Srisawat/Shutterstock;
17 iStockphoto/Thinkstock; 18 digitalreflections/Shutterstock;
19t tepic, b TFoxFoto/both Shutterstock; 20t Ewan Chesser,
b Malgorzata Kistryn/both Shutterstock; 21t Andresr, b James Laurie/
both Shutterstock; 22 Dorling Kindersley RF/Thinkstock;
23 iStockphoto/Thinkstock
Cover Dudarev Mikhail/Shutterstock

DAD0507
052013
9 8 7 6 5 4 3 2 1

Contents

My World

I am a cow. I live on a dairy farm
with lots of other cows.
Here are some of my herd.

In summer, we live outdoors.
We graze on grass in the fields.

**Cows graze
for up to eight
hours a day.**

4

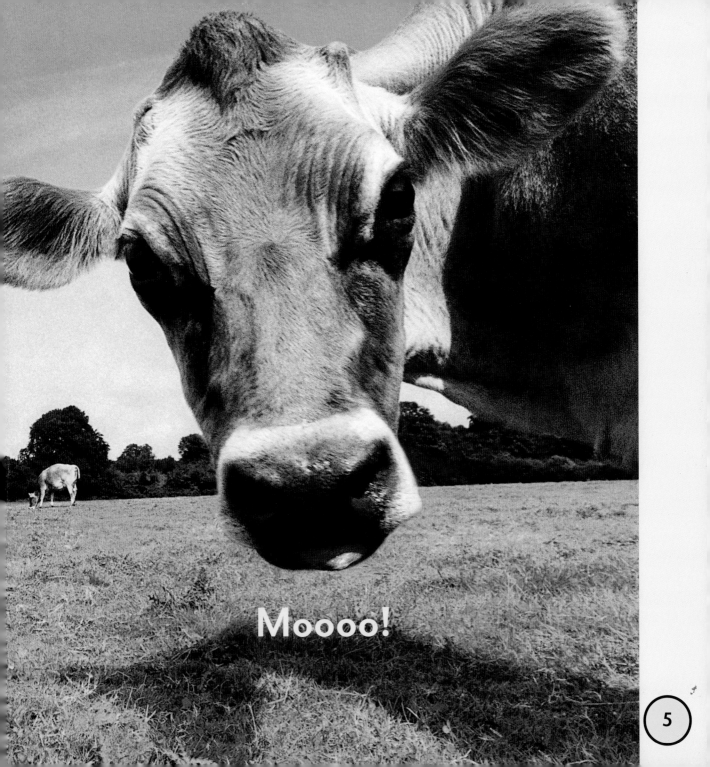

Moooo!

Changing Seasons

In the hot sun, we rest in the shade of trees in the pasture.

Cows don't sleep for long, but they like a comfortable spot to rest.

In winter, we shelter in the barn.
The straw helps to keep us warm.

Top to Toe

A cow's long tail can swipe at irritating insects.

Swishhh!

Most cows have a coat of black, brown, or white hair.

We can walk through slippery mud or over rough stones with our strong hooves.

Some male and female cows have horns.

Who Looks After Us?

Our spacious barn is warm and dry. The farmer keeps it clean, and makes sure we have enough to eat.

A vet visits regularly to keep us healthy and clip our hooves.

This feeder is full of clean hay for the cows to eat.

11

Time to Eat

Munch!

12

Our favorite foods are grass, hay, and leaves. In winter, we eat cereals and vitamins, too.

I move my head to tear leaves from the ground. A long tongue helps me to chew.

13

Cows and Calves

Dairy cows have a baby, called a calf, once a year. A bull is used to breed them.

Slurp

Newborn calves drink their mother's milk. Some calves are bottle-fed.

A young calf drinks about one gallon of milk every day.

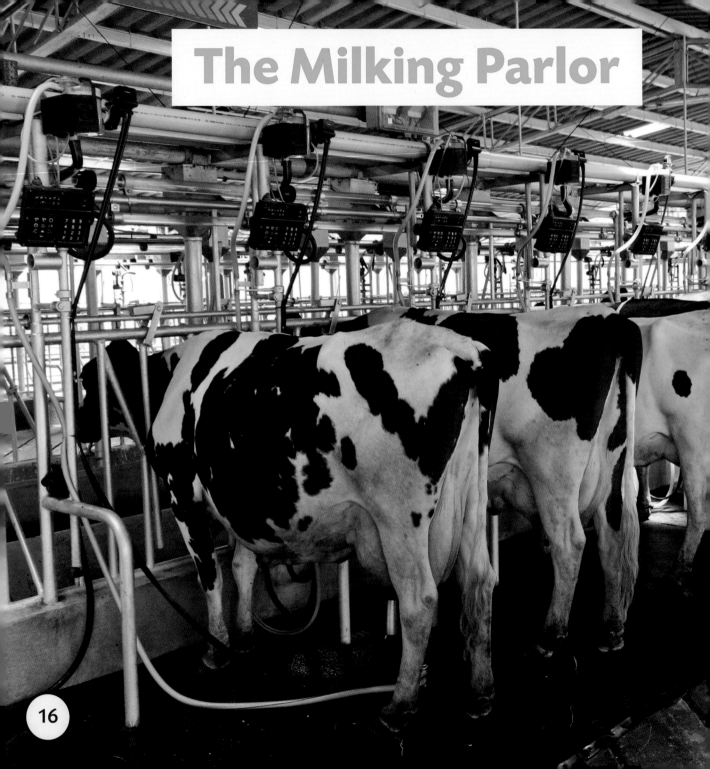

The Milking Parlor

We go to the milking parlor twice a day. The farmer puts milking machines on our udders.

The milk is stored in a cold tank before trucks take it away to be sold.

In the past, cows were milked by hand.

Dairy cows make up to eight gallons of milk every day!

Farm Produce

Cows are farmed for their milk, meat, and leather. Their milk is used to make dairy products, such as butter, cheese, and yogurt.

Herefords are bred for their meat, called beef.

Holsteins produce a lot of milk.

Jersey cows are smaller, but their milk is creamier.

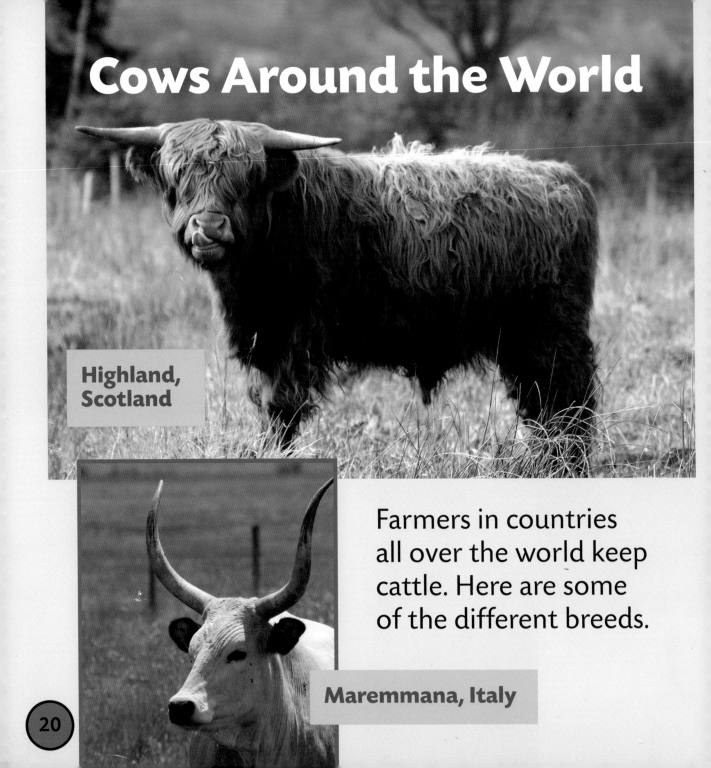

Cows Around the World

Highland, Scotland

Farmers in countries all over the world keep cattle. Here are some of the different breeds.

Maremmana, Italy

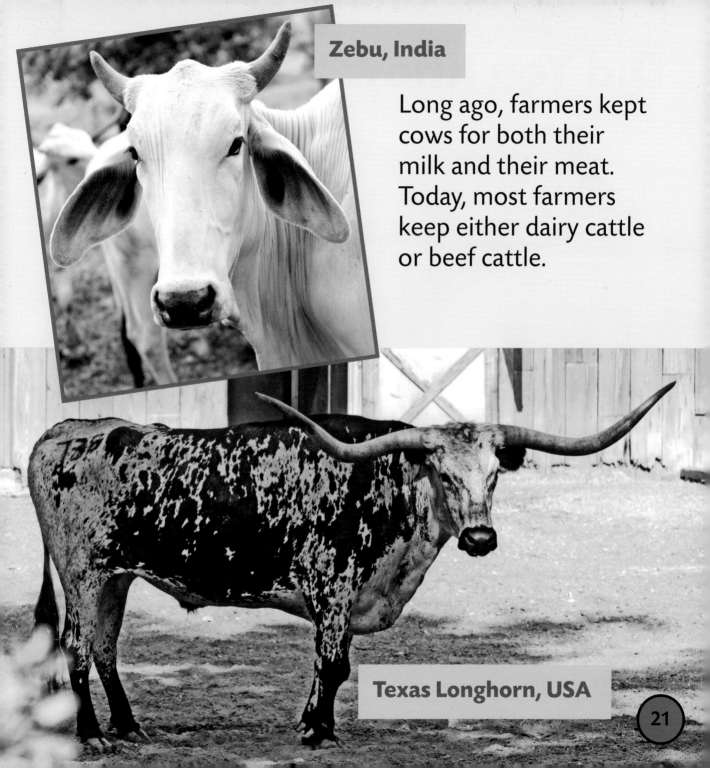

Zebu, India

Long ago, farmers kept cows for both their milk and their meat. Today, most farmers keep either dairy cattle or beef cattle.

Texas Longhorn, USA

Did You Know?

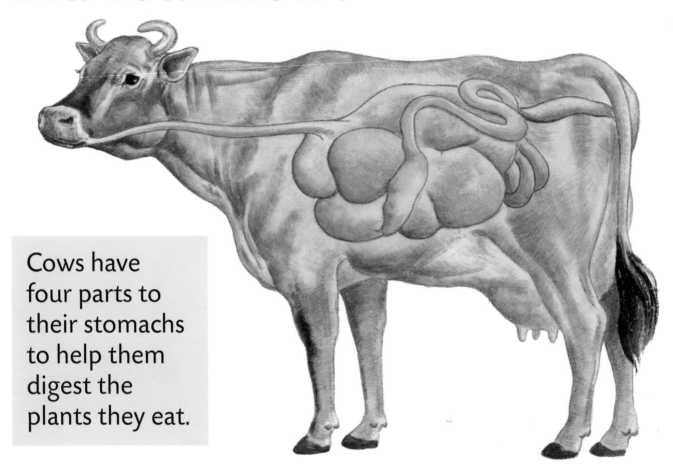

Cows have four parts to their stomachs to help them digest the plants they eat.

A cow has no top teeth at the front of its mouth.

Dairy cows need to drink lots of water: up to 50 gallons of water a day – that's about a bathtub full!

A cow moves its jaw and tongue up to 60,000 times a day to chew its food. All that chewing makes about 25 gallons of saliva.

Useful Words

bull
A male cow.

graze
Animals graze when they eat grass.

herd
A group of animals that live together.

leather
A material made from the skin of an animal.

pasture
Land used for grazing.

Index

Web Links

www.moomilk.com
www.sites.ext.vt.edu/virtualfarm/dairy/dairy.html
www://agriculture-4-u.co.uk/pages/Livestock/Dairy/milking.php
www.animalcorner.co.uk/farm/cows/cow_about.html
www.kidcyber.com.au/topics/farmcows.htm